THE YOUNG PRODUCER'S VIDEO BOOK

HOW TO WRITE, DIRECT, AND SHOOT YOUR OWN VIDEO

By Nancy Bentley and Donna W. Guthrie

Illustrated by Katy Keck Arnsteen

The Millbrook Press • Brookfield, Connecticut

This book is
dedicated to all
students who live
in the video age
and want to be
a part of it.

We acknowledge these people for their kind and generous supply of information and inspiration:
Kim Green and Doug Burwell, Media Production Specialists, Colorado Springs School District
#11; Hal Hildebrand, Production Engineer, Colorado Springs School District #11; Steve
Antonuccio, Director of Media, Pikes Peak Library District, Colorado Springs, Colorado.

Published by The Millbrook Press
2 Old New Milford Road, Brookfield, Connecticut 06804

Library of Congress Cataloging-in-Publication Data
Bentley, Nancy.
The young producer's video book: how to write, direct, and shoot
your own video/by Donna Guthrie, Nancy Bentley, and Katy Keck Arnsteen;
illustrated by Katy Keck Arnsteen.
p. cm.
Includes bibliographical references (p.   ) and index.
Summary: Provides step-by-step instructions on how to develop an idea,
write a script, handle a video camera, and edit the tape to produce a video.
ISBN 1-56294-566-1 (lib. bdg.) ISBN 1-56294-688-9 (pbk.)
1. Video recordings—Production and direction—Juvenile literature.
[1. Video recordings—Production and direction.] I. Bentley, Nancy.
II. Arnsteen, Katy Keck. III. Title.
PN1992.94.G88 1995   791.45'0232—dc20   94-48300   CIP   AC

TABLE OF CONTENTS

INTRODUCTION

Since the beginning of time, people have told stories. The first storytellers used their voices, body movements, and musical instruments to make their stories interesting and believable. But the storytellers could only share their stories with a few people at a time.

Once paper and pens were created, stories could be written down, illustrated, and shared by many people. The storyteller did not have to be present for the story to be enjoyed.

When film was invented, motion was added to pictures. But filmmaking requires a lot of equipment and is expensive.

Now you can use videotape to combine pictures, sound, and motion to become a modern storyteller. Videotape is inexpensive, portable, and easy to use. You can share your stories with family and friends, classmates and neighbors. This book is a step-by-step guide to telling your stories on videotape.

It will help you to:

ORGANIZE YOUR IDEAS

WRITE YOUR SCRIPT

SCHEDULE YOUR PRODUCTION

CREATE YOUR VERY OWN VIDEO PROGRAM

HOW ARE VIDEOS DIFFERENT FROM BOOKS?

A book is written and read.	A video is produced and viewed.
In some books your imagination creates pictures.	In a video the pictures are always created for you.
In a book the pictures you see are still.	In a video the pictures move.
A book is created by putting words on paper.	A video is created by putting sounds and pictures on magnetic tape.
A book can be read anywhere.	A video must be viewed on a machine.

So when do you use your imagination?

You use your imagination when you create and visualize your story.

TYPES OF VIDEOS

SEE
HEAR
FEEL

In a good video,
the pictures we see
and the sounds we hear
produce strong emotions.

Think in pictures, see in color,
Make your story go.
Show your facts with movement
In your vid-e-o!

Hear the voices, add the music,
Listen to the show.
Tell the facts with power
In your aud-i-o.

Make your viewers feel the facts,
Put them in the know.
Have the story grab them.
They'll stand and shout "Brav-o!"

There are two types of videos: fiction and nonfiction.

FICTION VIDEOS

A fiction video is a made-up story about real or imaginary people and events.

The rules for creating a good fiction video are the same as the rules for writing a good story.

1. The story or video must have characters we care about.

2. The story or video must have a setting that tells the viewer where and when the story is taking place.

3. The story or video must have a problem that characters can solve.

4. The story or video must have a beginning, a middle, and an end.

Camera! Lights! Action!
Add motion to the sound.
Create characters and actions
That amuse, amaze, astound.

Here are some types of fiction videos you might want to try:

AN ADAPTATION

An adaptation is a video script based on a story, a book, a play, or an article.

Adaptations are fun because they give you a chance to use your imagination. Look for a story that has a simple setting, strong characters, and lots of action.

Write a brief summary of the plot and identify the main message of the story. Try to do this in one sentence so that you have a clear idea of what your adaptation is about.

Then, jot down the names and profiles for each character. Next, create a script of one scene in the story by writing what you see the characters do and what you hear the characters say.

CHARACTER PROFILES:

GOLDILOCKS: Blond-haired, curious little girl who doesn't respect people's property.

BABY BEAR: A picky eater who has a favorite chair, a favorite bowl, and a favorite bed.

SCRIPT FORM:

BABY BEAR (angrily)
Who's sleeping in my bed?
GOLDILOCKS (sleepily)
Is it time for dinner?

AN EXPERIMENTAL VIDEO

An experimental video uses familiar tools to produce an unusual effect.

An experimental video challenges the viewer to see things in a new way. But remember, you are creating a story. It must have a beginning, a middle, and an end or the video will be boring or confusing to the viewer.

You can create an experimental film by:

- *Changing the film speed.* Perhaps you could shoot part of the film in slow motion.

- *Varying the camera angles.* Try standing on a chair or lying on your back when you film the action. This will give the viewer a different point of view.

- *Altering the music.* Experiment with different types and tempos of music to see how they change the mood of your story. For example, Peruvian flutes or steel drums can add a soothing or dramatic effect.

- *Using unusual lighting.* Try using sharp contrasts rather than normal lighting. Extremes in lighting give the viewer a sense of mystery and suspense.

- *Using a handheld camera.* Videos shot using handheld cameras give the viewer a feeling of being part of the action.

IDEAS FOR FICTION VIDEOS:

1 A MUSIC VIDEO WITH A STORY CREATED TO YOUR FAVORITE SONG.

2 A GAME SHOW VIDEO USING SUPERHEROES AS THE CONTESTANTS.

3 A VIDEO OF YOUR FAMILY AND HOUSE FROM YOUR DOG'S-EYE VIEW.

4 A COMEDY SHOW WITH YOUR FRIENDS AS CHARACTERS.

5 AN ORIGINAL MYSTERY CALLED "THE CASE OF THE DISAPPEARING PRINCIPAL."

6 A historical COOKING SHOW WITH GEORGE WASHINGTON BAKING HIS FAVORITE CHERRY PIE.

NONFICTION VIDEOS

A nonfiction video tells a true story of real events or conveys information. The rules for writing a good nonfiction video are the same as the rules for writing a good report.

1. A nonfiction video must have a purpose. Decide what you want your audience to know about the subject.

2. A nonfiction video must be supported by facts. It must answer the questions who, what, where, when, why, and how.

3. A nonfiction video must have a catchy lead, or hook, at the beginning.

4. A nonfiction video can try to change the viewer's point of view.

5. A nonfiction video can explain a complicated idea in a simple way.

Here are some types of nonfiction videos you can make:

Camera, lights and action!
Add motion to the sound.
Give facts and information.
Report the truth you've found.

A HOW-TO VIDEO

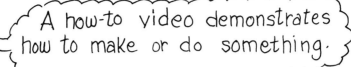

A how-to video demonstrates how to make or do something.

Your how-to video script should break the subject down into easy steps. Before shooting, arrange your materials and equipment in the order they will be used. Your crew will need to practice the best camera angles and shots. This type of video is best done with two cameras: one for close-ups, the other to show the work area and the finished project.

How-to videos can be divided into three parts. Part 1 invites the viewer to learn something new. Part 2 explains each step of the project. Part 3 presents the final product.

A COMMERCIAL

A commercial is an advertisement broadcast on television or radio.

When you write a commercial, you're trying to persuade the viewer to buy something. Advertisers base their commercials on people's five basic needs: shelter, clothing, food, love, and self-esteem. Choose one of these needs and emphasize it to promote your product.

Your commercial should have a strong hook at the beginning to grab the viewers' attention. In the middle, show the product in use and give reasons why the viewer would want it. At the end, tell the viewer where your product can be found and how much it is.

A different kind of commercial is a PSA, a public service announcement. In 30 seconds or less, a PSA provides information about community groups or on topics such as public health and safety. You can try to submit your PSA to your local cable or public television station, which might air it for no charge.

The clock is ticking! Most commercials are 30 or 60 seconds. A 30-second commercial is approximately 60 words long, and a 60-second commercial is about 120 words.

A VIDEO REPORT

A video report presents a topic using factual information from written and visual sources.

A video report uses the elements of motion, sound, and multimedia to present a factual topic. It can either be a documentary or a docudrama.

Before you write your video script, limit the subject. Collect the facts, organize your materials, make an outline, and summarize the information. You will need to do extensive research. In addition to printed sources, gather visual materials like photographs, slides, posters, postcards, and film on your topic.

Divide your script into three parts. Part 1 should establish a setting and hook the viewer. You might want to begin by asking a question or presenting a little-known fact. Part 2 presents the facts: who, what, where, when, why, and how. Part 3 summarizes the information and draws a conclusion.

A documentary is a factual account of real people, places, or events, based on historical and scientific information.

A docudrama is based on historical fact but uses imagined action and dialogue.

A VIDEO BIOGRAPHY

> A video biography is a video history of a person's life.

A video biography is a good way to highlight important moments in someone's life. Choose someone who is celebrating a birthday or anniversary or who has achieved a goal. In the video, present new information or insights about this person.

Your script should have three parts. In Part 1, focus on the person's background. Use old photographs, slides, and music to establish a mood. In Part 2, give information about the person and his or her accomplishments. This can be done through interviews with family and friends.

In Part 3, show the person today. Include a portion of a special event such as your grandmother blowing out the candles on her birthday cake. Ask the subject for personal reflections about his or her life. A video biography is a priceless addition to your family history.

> Prepare a list of open-ended questions in advance of your interviews.

Closed-ended questions are answered by yes or no. Open-ended questions encourage an explanation.

Closed-ended question: Do you like peanut butter? Answer: Yes!

Open-ended question: From your experience, why shouldn't people drop banana peels in the kitchen? Answer: Well, one day when my friend Flo came over…

IDEAS FOR NONFICTION VIDEOS:

1 A VIDEO YEARBOOK OF THE MEMBERS OF YOUR CLASS.

2 A TRAVEL VIDEO SHOWING THE HISTORICAL BUILDINGS IN YOUR TOWN.

3 A SCIENCE VIDEO ABOUT CARING FOR A WOUNDED PEREGRINE FALCON.

4 A VIDEO REPORT ABOUT THE ART OF GEORGIA O'KEEFE.

5 A DOCUMENTARY SHOWING PET ADOPTIONS AT THE HUMANE SOCIETY.

6 A PSA AGAINST SMOKING TO BE SHOWN DURING "ANTI-SMOKING WEEK."

THE SEVEN STEPS TO VIDEO PRODUCTION

Making a video involves lots of people, called a crew. You will be the person in charge, but things will happen that you can't control. Think of this as an adventure. Stay flexible and be creative. Focus on your goal but leave room for new ideas and suggestions from your crew.

The process of making a video is divided into three stages: Pre-Production (before), Production (during), and Post-Production (after). These three stages can be divided into seven steps:

PRE-PRODUCTION
Step 1:
- Choose the crew.
- Brainstorm the idea.
- Decide the type of video.
Step 2:
- Do the research.
- Use the camera.
Step 3:
- Write the script.
- Plan the storyboard.

PRODUCTION
Step 4:
- Direct the talent.
Step 5:
- Tape the story.

POST-PRODUCTION
Step 6:
- Edit the video.
Step 7:
- Present the show.

PRE - PRODUCTION

This is the first stage, when you

Choose the crew

Brainstorm the idea

FICTION? NONFICTION?

Decide the type of video

LIBRARY

SLIDES . PHOTOS

INTERVIEWS

HISTORICAL LOCATIONS

Research the topic

Use the camera

Write the script

STORYBOARD

Create the storyboard

CHOOSE THE CREW

It's difficult to make a video by yourself. There are too many jobs for one person to do, so gather a crew.

The *producer* makes all the arrangements and organizes the people and the equipment.

The *scriptwriter* creates the outline, the rough draft, a storyboard, dialogue, and the final draft.

The *director* works with the actors and coordinates the camera shots.

The *camera person* is responsible for the camera and lighting and for final editing of the film.

The *sound person* is responsible for music and microphones.

The *actors*, or *talent*, are the people who are in front of the camera being filmed.

Sometimes people can do more than one job. But don't ask anyone to do too much!

20

BRAINSTORM AND THEN DECIDE THE TOPIC

- Meet with your crew to plan the video.

- Talk about possible topics and gather as many different ideas as you can.

- Think about the equipment you have available.

- Be sure the type of video you make fits your subject. If your topic is humorous, treat it lightly. If your story is serious, present the facts clearly and plainly.

Decide the type of video you want to make.
Will it be fiction or nonfiction?

DO THE RESEARCH

Start at the library to research the topic of your video. Read books, encyclopedias, magazines, and newspapers.

Listen to taped interviews, special sound effects, and music.

Examine computer databases, photographs, slides, and maps.

You can visit the places where events happened and interview people who were on the scene or who have expert firsthand information.

USE THE CAMERA

In a book, your imagination creates the pictures.
In a video, you create the pictures with your camera.
Develop your video "eye" by learning what the camera can do.
Think in pictures. Each picture is a shot.

POINT OF VIEW

My world is getting larger.
I'm seeing things anew.
Looking through my camera,
I've got a brand-new view!

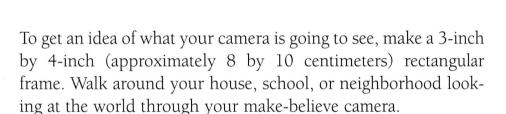

To get an idea of what your camera is going to see, make a 3-inch by 4-inch (approximately 8 by 10 centimeters) rectangular frame. Walk around your house, school, or neighborhood looking at the world through your make-believe camera.

This is what the human eye sees.

This is what the camera's eye sees.

BASIC CAMERA SHOTS

A shot begins when you press the record button on your camera and ends when you release the button.

A shot can go on too long. When it does, it's BORING! Try to limit your shot to fifteen seconds. To make a scene more interesting, combine these three basic shots:

- Wide shot

- Medium shot

- Close-up shot

WIDE
SHOT

The *wide shot* (also called *long shot*) shows the big picture from side to side and front to back.

It includes several people in a large area. It can answer the question "Where am I?"

In the first minute of a good video, the viewer sees where the action takes place through a wide shot called an establishing shot. An establishing shot shows the setting and sets the mood for the video.

MEDIUM SHOT

A *medium shot* moves in a little closer to the scene. It shows people from the waist up. Most television interview shows use medium shots.

CLOSE-UP SHOT

A *close-up shot* moves in even closer and focuses on a single thing, such as a person's face.

Use this shot when you want to add tension and excitement.

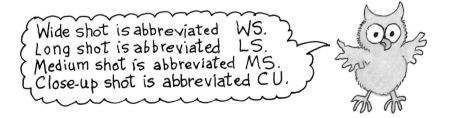

Wide shot is abbreviated WS.
Long shot is abbreviated LS.
Medium shot is abbreviated MS.
Close-up shot is abbreviated CU.

CAMERA MOVEMENTS

Here's how you can use camera movements to make your video more interesting.

Tilt: Move the camera up and down. Think of nodding your head "yes."

Tilt up means shoot higher.

Tilt down means shoot lower.

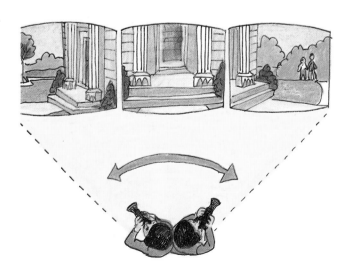

Pan: Move the camera back and forth. Think of shaking your head "no."

Pan left means move the camera toward your left.

Pan right means move the camera toward your right.

Zoom: Make the picture look closer or farther away; turn the camera lens but don't move the camera. *Zoom in* means turn the lens to make the picture look closer and bigger. *Zoom out* means turn the lens to make the picture look farther away and smaller.

Pedestal adjusts the height of the camera's lens.
Pedestal up means move the camera higher.
Pedestal down means move the camera lower.

CAMERA ANGLES

You can make the audience feel different emotions by the way you angle your camera.

Three ways to angle your camera are:

EYE LEVEL   HIGH ANGLE   LOW ANGLE

An *eye-level shot* is the way most people see the world. Hold the camera at head and shoulder level. Use this angle to make the subject look normal.

For a *high-angle shot*, hold the camera above the subject's head. It makes the subject look small, weak, or afraid.

In a *low-angle shot*, the camera is held below the subject. It makes the subject look tall, strong, or scary.

TRANSITIONS

The move from one scene to another is called a *transition*. Transitions are the connecting links in your program.

Common transitions are:

Cut: A cut is a sudden change in camera angles or viewpoint. Remember to match the action and camera direction so that your shots don't appear choppy.

Dissolve: A dissolve happens when a picture slowly fades while another picture slowly appears in its place.

Fade: A fade is a type of dissolve in which the picture slowly fades to black or begins black and fades into a picture.

Black-out: In a black-out, the talent walks toward the camera, blocking out all the light. The next scene begins when the talent walks away from the camera into a scene.

WRITE THE SCRIPT

STEP 3

Stories on video are viewed on a screen, not read. So when writing a script for video, you must see in your mind the pictures that tell the story. Keep your script simple. Imagine that you are going to tell the story without saying a single word.

PLOTTING

Think of a video as a three-act play. There's a beginning (Act 1), a middle (Act 2), and an end (Act 3). In Act 1, introduce the

In a video story there are two important moments when the character must act and the story is pushed forward. These are called plot points. They occur at the end of Act 1 and the end of Act 2.

main character and his or her problem.

In Act 2, the character tries to solve his or her problem. This is where most of the action takes place. In Act 3, the audience finds out if the character has been successful and if he or she has

BEGINNING
ACT 1

PLOT
POINTS

MIDDLE
ACT 2

PLOT
POINTS

END
ACT 3

CHARACTERS

Write a brief description of all the characters. This is called a pro-file. It will help the actors and director know what the characters should look like and what they feel and think. Each time a new character is introduced, be sure to describe him or her in your script, both inside and out. Your character profile might look like this:

> Harold: A twelve-year-old boy who loves snakes and is afraid of girls. He could be very handsome if he stood up straight and smiled more.

CHARACTER MOVEMENTS

You can tell a lot about characters by watching the way they move. In a video story, think about how your characters will move across the screen. Write suggestions to your actors in the script. Keep them short and concise. Here is an example:

> Harold talks to his favorite snake as he walks down the street. He bumps into the pretty girl next door who is holding her pet ferret.

A gesture or motion that the character does again and again helps the viewer understand the character's personality.

SETTING

The setting is the time and place when and where the actions happen. Time can be the time of day or the date. Changes in time and setting are called scenes.

In a video script, the setting directions are at the beginning of each scene. Setting directions will help the crew gather props and costumes and prepare the lighting. In your script, your setting directions might look like this:

Abbreviate interior as INT. exterior as EXT.

INT. HAROLD'S ROOM—EARLY MORNING

EXT. OUTSIDE ON THE WAY TO SCHOOL —DAY

DIALOGUE

Dialogue is the words that the characters speak to one another. Video scriptwriters use adverbs to tell the actors and actresses how to speak their lines. In your script, your dialogue directions might look like this:

REBECCA (curiously): Where did you get that necklace?

HAROLD (proudly): It's not a necklace. It's Freddy, my pet snake. I'm taking it to school for hobby day.

REBECCA: That's where we're going.

Rebecca lifts up the lid on her basket and a furry ferret head pops out. Harold drops the snake into his shirt and buttons up his coat. He hurries off.

A voice-over is when you hear but do not see the narrator. Use VO as an abbreviation.

STORYBOARD

Now that you know about camera shots you're ready to make a storyboard.

Storyboarding is the next step in planning your video.

Take your outline and use what you know about camera movements and angles to plan the actual camera shots.

Divide a piece of paper in half. On the left-hand side of the page, write in order the things the audience will SEE.

On the right-hand side of the page, write the sounds the audience will HEAR.

In the middle, draw simple stick figures and simple shapes to show step-by-step what your video will look like. Don't worry about being an artist.

On the video side of your storyboard, write the actual camera shots, such as medium shot, wide shot, close-up shot.

Include your camera movements, such as zoom out, pan right, tilt down. Also include the transitions, such as cut, dissolve, fade to black, or fade from black.

On the audio, show when music plays, when people talk, and when natural sounds or sound effects are heard.

Using notebook paper, make a storyboard on the wall. This gives the whole crew an idea of what your video will look like.

THE PRODUCTION STAGE

Now that you have finished the pre-production stage, you are ready to pick up the camera. This stage is called production. During the production stage you

- decide on the director
- work with the talent
- arrange the set
- position the lights
- review the camera shot list
- set up the microphones
- tape the action

EQUIPMENT LIST

Before you start shooting, it is a good idea to make a list of all the equipment you need.

Production Gear Checklist:

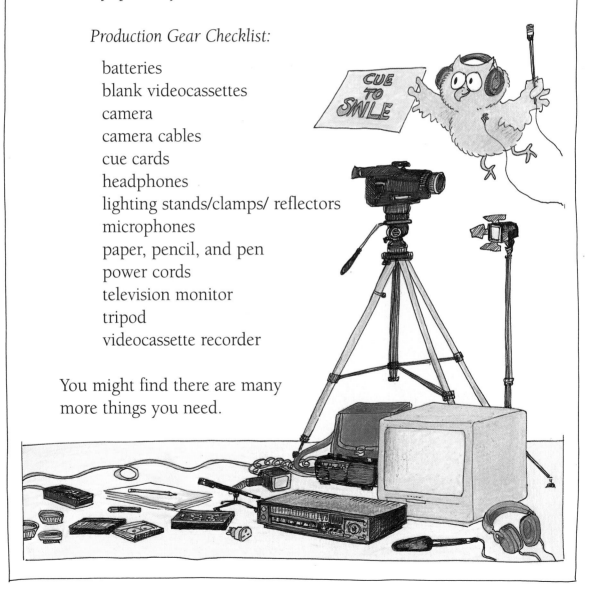

- batteries
- blank videocassettes
- camera
- camera cables
- cue cards
- headphones
- lighting stands/clamps/ reflectors
- microphones
- paper, pencil, and pen
- power cords
- television monitor
- tripod
- videocassette recorder

You might find there are many more things you need.

DIRECT THE TALENT

During the production stage the director is in charge.

The director's job is to guide the people in front of and behind the camera. If the video needs two cameras, the director can use a television monitor to coordinate the camera shots.

The director can say:

TALENT

Talent is a word that describes the people in front of the camera.

TIME

Give the talent plenty of time to rehearse so that once the cameras are on, everyone will know his or her part and the action will go smoothly.

CLOTHES

Ask the talent to wear soft colors like greens, blues, grays, or pastels. The talent shouldn't wear the color white, shiny jewelry, or bold stripes or plaids because they're visually distracting.

POSTURE

Ask the talent not to sway, wiggle, touch their faces, or play with the microphone cord.

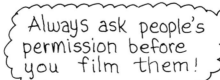

Always ask people's permission before you film them!

CUE CARDS

If your talent has something to say in your video, make *cue cards*.

1. Make cue cards out of poster board: 15 inches wide by 30 to 40 inches long (approximately 40 by 75 to 100 centimeters). Write with a black felt-tip pen.

2. Use all capital letters.

3. Use no more than five words per line and no more than ten lines per card.

4. Place cards at a distance of 10 to 12 feet (3 to 3.6 meters) from the talent. Make sure the letters are 1 1/2 inches (3.75 centimeters) high and easy to read. Ask the talent how close the cards need to be.

5. Hold the card being read level with the camera lens. Smoothly position the next card level with the camera lens. This takes practice.

6. Give the talent a chance to rehearse using cue cards.

BLOCKING

Before you shoot your video, the talent must practice when and where to move. The planning of these movements in front of the camera is called *blocking*.

ALWAYS PUT PEOPLE OR OBJECTS CLOSE TO EACH OTHER.

KEEP OBJECTS CLOSE TO THE TALENT'S FACE.

BLOCK TOWARD AND AWAY FROM THE CAMERA TO CREATE DEPTH.

BLOCK TALENT IN EITHER AN L OR V SHAPE TO KEEP THE PICTURE INTERESTING.

INTERVIEWS

Make your information video more interesting by using interviews. During an interview, position the camera at shoulder level. This gives the viewer the impression that you're having a conversation. If your subject is much taller or shorter than you, you should both be seated for filming.

When interviewing someone on video:

 PREPARE A LIST OF QUESTIONS AHEAD OF TIME

 MAKE THE PERSON FEEL COMFORTABLE

 LOOK DIRECTLY AT THE PERSON WHEN YOU TALK

 ASK OPEN-ENDED QUESTIONS

 BE POLITE

Before you tape the interview, role-play all the questions with your friends. This is good practice in using a camera and microphone.

CAMERA SHOT LIST

Before you begin to film, use your storyboard as a guide to make a *camera shot list*. This list will tell the camera person the order and kind of shot to take. This makes it easy for the camera person to move from shot to shot.

CAMERA SHOT LIST

DIRECTOR: Wendy Lin
CAMERA PERSON: Marcos Rodriguez
CAMERA ASSISTANT: Keisha Washington
DATE: April 25
TIME: 10:00 A.M.
LOCATION: Media Center

PROGRAM: The Un-peeling of Hungry Flo

1.	WS	of Flo in kitchen
2.	MS	Flo goes to cupboard and takes out peanut butter (PAN·LEFT)
3.	MS	Flo walks to refrigerator and gets loaf of bread (continue PAN)
4.	CU	Flo opens drawer, takes knife. (TILT)
5.	CU	Flo takes a banana from fruit basket. (ZOOM·IN)
6.	MS	Flo carries things back to counter (PAN·RIGHT)
7.	MS	Flo sniffs bread. (ZOOM·IN)
8.	MS	Flo spreads peanut butter on bread.
9.	MS	Flo unpeels banana.
10.	WS	banana peel falls on floor. (TILT·DOWN)
11.	MS	Flo slices banana on sandwich (TILT·UP)
12.	MS	Flo takes a bite of sandwich and steps back
13.	WS	Flo slips on banana peel and falls down.
14.	CU	Flo's face. (TILT·DOWN)

TAPE THE STORY

STEP 5

Each camera is different. Read the directions and learn the controls. Practice with the camera before you make your video.

USING A TRIPOD

A tripod is a stand with three legs. It is an important piece of equipment because it holds the camera steady. Practice your camera movements with the tripod.

SHOOTING OUTSIDE

Find a convenient power outlet or use batteries.

Choose a quiet place.

Don't stand next to a glass building. It will reflect light back on the camera.

HOW TO USE A HANDHELD CAMERA

Here are some tips on how to use your camera without a tripod:

- Stand with your feet apart, toes out.
- Bend your knees to remain flexible.
- Lean against something sturdy, like a tree or a fence.
- Glide forward on your toes to avoid jerky pictures on your tape.
- Keep the camera at shoulder level to avoid jumpy shots.

SPREAD FEET.

BEND KNEES.

USE SUPPORT.

GLIDE FORWARD.

AVOID JUMPS.

COMPOSITION

1.

Under "the rule of thirds," the picture is divided into three equal parts, horizontally or vertically.

2.

Horizons and heads belong *not* in the center but one third up or down.

3.

When the talent is looking to the right, leave open space on the right. If the talent is looking to the left, leave open space on the left. This is called "lead room."

4.

Avoid large areas of blank screen.

5.

Watch for things "growing out" of your talent's head.

6.

Create depth in your shots by using props.

Good composition directs the viewer's eye to the important things in the picture.

7.

Instead of shooting your subject straight on like a mug shot, have them turn a bit to the left or right.

8.

Check for shadows. Make sure they are not in the picture.

9.

The talent may enter the picture from the same side if they enter as a group.

10.

Make sure people keep moving in the same direction when they enter and exit the picture.

11.

Think about background. Don't let it get in the way.

12.

Keep the camera level and in focus.

LIGHTING

Good lighting makes the subject look three-dimensional, not flat.

In video production a basic rule is to always have three lights:

The *key light* is the brightest light that shines on the person in front of the camera.

The *back light* is placed above and behind the talent to give the picture depth.

The *fill light* adds more light to the subject but is not as bright as the key light or the back light.

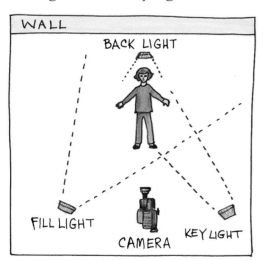

If you are outside or in a room with many large windows, the sun is the key light.

Be consistent - shoot all of a scene either in the sun or in the shade.

Check to see if you have enough light by shooting for a few seconds.

MICROPHONES

What you hear on your video is as important as what you see. Use a good microphone when recording. Most video recorders have a built-in microphone. If you use an in-camera microphone, make sure you're close enough to the talent. Check by having the talent speak and see how far back you can stand and still hear them.

Sometimes the built-in mike picks up more sound than you want. For quiet situations the most common microphones are the lavaliere and the handheld mike.

A *lavaliere* is a small microphone that can be attached to clothing. Make sure nothing brushes up against it or the noise will be recorded.

The *handheld microphone* can be passed back and forth but it will pick up noise. In an interview, hold it halfway between the two speakers.

The talent should
- Hold the microphone 6 to 12 inches (15 to 30 centimeters) from his or her mouth
- Speak *over* the microphone, not into it
- Move the microphone slowly

SLIDES AND PICTURES

If you are doing a history or travel video, photographs and slides are a quick and easy way to journey through time and space.

Your library will help you locate posters, slides, or pictures for your video. You may need to get permission to photograph or videotape some of these materials.

If you have access to electronic editing equipment, prepare all your slides and photographs on a separate videotape. You can add them onto your master tape during the editing process.

ANIMATION

Animation is a technique that makes objects appear to move. You can use clay, puppets, or small toys. Animation creates an illusion of movement and a feeling that the objects are alive. If you have a videocamera with animation capability, you can record a few frames each time you press the button.

Animation steps:

Mount your camera on a tripod.
Light your object well.
Videotape the object, a few frames at a time.
Make a small change in the object's position.
Videotape again.

To animate a piece of artwork:

Mount your videocamera on
   a tripod.
Set up a blank piece of paper
   on a low table.
Light your paper.
Draw a few lines on the paper.
Videotape progress.
Draw a few more lines.
Videotape again.
Continue until the picture is finished.
When you play it back, the picture will seem
   to draw itself.

THE POST-PRODUCTION STAGE

During the post-production stage you

- create a camera log sheet
- create graphics
- add the sound track
- edit tapes
- show the video

This is the last chance to polish your video.

EDIT THE VIDEO

A camera log sheet is a list of camera shots in the order they were taken. Sometimes during the filming, you make a shot you hadn't planned on or the talent misses a word and must repeat the line.

The camera automatically records the amount of time each shot takes. During playback, use the counter button to record these numbers on your camera log sheet.

An assistant can help the camera person by writing down the counter numbers. This will help you keep track of the good shots for easy editing.

PROGRAM TITLE : The Unpeeling of Flo
CAMERA PERSON : Marcos Rodriguez
CAMERA ASSISTANT : Keisha Washington

BEGINNING	END	LOCATION	VIDEO
100	130	Int. Kitchen	WS of Flo in Kitchen
130	135	same	MS Flo goes to cupboard
135	140	same	take 1 WS of Flo drops bread
140	145	same	take 2 WS of Flo getting bread from refrig.

GRAPHICS

Graphics are titles, captions, and credits that give your videotape a finished look. There are three times you can create and add graphics to your video: before the filming, during the filming, and after the filming.

Before the filming, create your own art-work by using signs, photographs, books, maps, original art, or your own lettering. Use shelf paper for your credit list so you can roll it up and down. Calculate how long credits should remain on the screen by reading them to yourself at a normal reading speed.

During filming you can create titles from things you find on-site, like pebbles, rocks, shells, or street signs. When using these materials, make sure all the letters are approximately the same size so they can be read easily.

After filming, you can add titles and credits by using a computer or a *production mixer*.

* LIMIT THE WORDS
* MAKE THE TITLES FIT THE MOOD
* USE SIMPLE BOLD LETTERS

53

THE SOUND TRACK

The *sound track* consists of music, narration, and sound effects. It sets the mood and tone of your video.

    Music is usually heard at the beginning and end of a video. *Narration* is a voice off-camera telling the story. *Sound effects* are accents to the action, such as a crash, a whistle, or a scream.

    Three ways to make a sound track:

1. Record the music and sound effects live. If you're making a video of your brother's clarinet recital, record the music live using the camera's built-in microphone.

2. Prerecord your sound track onto an audiotape and play it during the filming. If you're making a music video, prerecord the song on an audiotape and play it during the filming.

3. Add music, narration, and sound effects during editing. If you're doing an anniversary video for your grandparents, combine an interview with pictures and music from their past. This type of sound track is best created with advanced editing equipment.

EDITING

Editing is the most important part of the post–production stage. You shape your audience's response by establishing a pace for your video. This is done by cutting, tightening, and ordering your shots.

During editing, you will use your storyboard and camera log sheet to create a final tape. This is also the time to add special effects and graphics.

There are three common ways to edit videotape.

ONE-CAMERA EDITING

If you have only one camera, you will need to edit "in camera."

You must take the shots in the exact sequence that you have planned. What you shoot is what you get for your final tape.

SCENE 1

START.

STOP SCENE BY PUSHING PAUSE BUTTON

SCENE 2

PUSH AGAIN TO START RECORDING.

STOP.

You must plan ahead and stick to your script.

If you make a mistake you can rewind the tape and shoot it again with a second "take." This is not easy to do and requires practice to avoid echo.

TAPE-TO-TAPE EDITING

You can use your video camera and your videotape recorder for tape-to-tape editing. Use your log sheet, storyboard, and video camera to review and choose the actions you want to save.

Place a blank tape into the videotape recorder. Run it for 30 seconds. Now copy the shots you want to use from the video camera onto the master tape. By stopping and starting you create a final version.

Each video camera and videotape recorder will be different and have different options. Ask an adult for training and help before you start to edit.

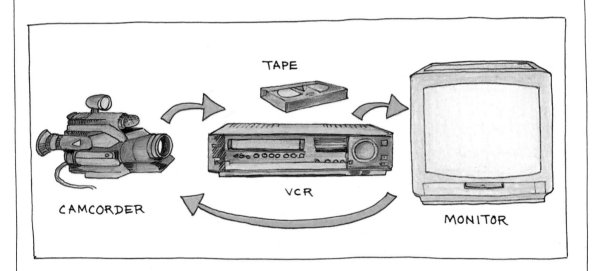

CAMCORDER   TAPE   VCR   MONITOR

COMPUTER EDITING

Using a computerized editing system is the most sophisticated way to edit videotapes. The system is designed to make a master tape by synchronizing several videotapes with music and special effects.

You can find these systems in professional studios, cable television stations, public libraries, and large school districts. A simplified home editing machine can be purchased at a camera or computer store.

Some systems have editing options like special graphics, *shattering* the picture, *melting* a picture, or *wiping* the picture off the screen.

Use your storyboard and log sheet to edit in your options and create your master tape.

SHATTER

MELT

WIPE

PRESENT THE SHOW

Now that you have a master videotape, you are ready to show it

- to friends and family
- in your class
- to the school librarian
- to the public librarian
- to your local cable television station
- in video contests

Now that you're a video producer, keep your eyes open for pictures, your ears open for dialogue, and your imagination open for new stories to tell!

STORYBOARD SAMPLE

VIDEO		AUDIO
Flo in kitchen WS INT. kitchen		MUSIC UNDER
Flo goes to cupboard takes out the peanut butter. MS - pan left		SOUND OF DOOR OPENING "I'm hungry."
She walks to the refrigerator and gets bread. MS - continue pan		SOUND OF THE REFRIGERATOR DOOR OPENING
Flo opens the drawer and takes out a knife. CU - tilt down		SOUND OF DRAWER SLIDING
She takes a banana from the fruit basket. CU - zoom in		"This should do it."
She carries things to kitchen counter. MS - pan right		FOOTSTEPS
She sniffs bread. MS - zoom in		SOUND OF SNIFFING.

VIDEO		AUDIO
Flo spreads peanut butter on the bread MS		"This needs a little something to make it great." SOUND OF JAR OPENING
Flo unpeels banana. MS		
Peel drops on floor. WS - tilt down		SOUND OF PEEL ON FLOOR "Thunk"
Flo slices banana onto the peanut butter. MS - tilt up		
She takes a bite and steps back. MS		DRUM ROLL
She slips on the banana peel. WS		CRASH MUSIC UP
Flo's face CU - tilt		MUSIC FULL

STORYBOARD FORM

VIDEO	AUDIO

CAMERA SHOT LIST FORM

CAMERA SHOT LIST

DIRECTOR: _____

CAMERA PERSON: _____

CAMERA ASSISTANT: _____

DATE: _____

TIME: _____

LOCATION: _____

PROGRAM: _____

CAMERA LOG SHEET

PROGRAM TITLE: _ _ _ _ _ _ _ _ _ _ _ _ _ _ _ _ _ _ _
CAMERA PERSON: _ _ _ _ _ _ _ _ _ _ _ _ _ _ _ _ _ _ _
CAMERA ASSISTANT: _ _ _ _ _ _ _ _ _ _ _ _ _ _ _ _ _

BEGINNING	END	LOCATION	VIDEO

INDEX